bad indian

bad indian

poems

J.C. Mehta

Brick Mantel Books
Saint Louis, Missouri

Copyright © 2020 J.C. Mehta

All rights reserved. No part of this book may be reproduced or transmitted in any form or by any means, electronic or mechanical, including photocopying, recording, or by any information storage and retrieval system, without permission in writing from the publisher.

Published by Brick Mantel Books, USA

Brick Mantel
BOOKS

www.BrickMantelBooks.com
info@BrickMantelBooks.com

An imprint of Pen & Publish, LLC
Saint Louis, Missouri
(314) 827-6567
www.PenandPublish.com

Print ISBN: 978-1-941799-76-5
eBook ISBN: 978-1-941799-77-2

Library of Congress Control Number: 2019954052

Printed on acid-free paper.

Thank you to Potlatch Fund and North Street Collective for your support in helping to bring this project to fruition.

For Shanti, whose heart is so big because ours, too, belong to you.

Introduction

Native American women are murdered at a higher rate per capita than any other demographic in the United States. It's a crisis that has led to the missing and murdered indigenous women (MMIW) movement. According to the US Department of Justice, Native women are murdered at a rate 10 times higher than the national average. The vast majority of these murders are by non-Native men. The Centers for Disease Control and Prevention (CDC) report that murder is the third most common cause of death for Native girls and women aged 10–24 and the fifth most common cause for those aged 25–34. This is nothing new. We have a long history and legacy of violence against Native peoples, and women in particular, in post-Colonial America.

The staggering missing and murder rates Native women face are just two telling disparities. Per capita, Native Americans rank first in child poverty, are the most likely to be killed by police officers, and Native women are incarcerated at a rate six times higher than our white counterparts. According to Indian Health Services, compared to the general population Native Americans face higher mortality rates from *every major cause* except Alzheimer's Disease. This includes heart disease, cancer, accidental injuries, diabetes, chronic lower respiratory disease, strokes, influenza and pneumonia, kidney disease, hypertension, and of course murder. Native Americans are 6.6 times more likely than the general population to die of alcohol-induced death and 4.6 times more likely to die of liver disease. The CDC reports that Native Americans also face a higher suicide rate per capita than any other demographic, and that rate has been steadily increasing. These statistics are founded in what Roxanne Dunbar-Ortiz calls "Settler Colonialism" which is based on imperialism and ultimately "a genocide policy."

A report by the Urban Indian Health Institute (UIHI) found that there were 5,712 MMIW cases reported in 2016, but only 116 of these cases were logged by the Department of Justice. The UIHI stresses that the reported cases are likely a severe "undercount."

MMIW is a movement in the US and Canada in response to what has become an epidemic. Support for MMIW is often represented by the wearing or display of red dresses as well as the painting of a hand (often red) across a Native woman's or girl's face. "No more stolen sisters" is a popular refrain that serves as a reminder of the thousands of Native girls and women who go missing or are murdered every year.

Here's what *everyone* can do to support the MMIW movement:

- Educate ourselves and others. The Coalition to Stop Violence Against Native Women and MMIW USA are great resources.
- Encourage congresspeople and senators to pass legislation to close legal loopholes that contribute to the disappearance and murder of Native girls and women.
- Participate in local #MMIW events and marches to raise awareness about this epidemic.

Contents

Do You See the Stars?	13
Bad Indian	14
Spring Frenzy	15
Pulitzer Prize Pig	16
An Anorexia Thing	17
The Wrong Kind of Indian	18
The Catamaran	19
Resurrection	20
The L Words	21
Love You More	22
Totem of You	23
Childhood	24
I Thought You Were Praying	25
Inside the Rosemary Bush	26
How I Like My Women	27
Men	28
Christmas Chai	29
Relief	30
Bouquet of the Body	31
Eating	32
Hush-Hush	33
Relativity	34
The Two Percent	35
How Dying Is Done	36
Rezervations	38
The Sweet Below the Bitter	40
Kitchen Volcanoes	41
Great Grace and Sharp Wings	42
The History in My Blood	43
Something Sweet	44
The Banana Plantation	45
mURDERED & mISSING iNDIGENOUS wOMEN	46
Place Settings	48
Constructing Carnage	49
Racing Camels	50
Gestation	52
Down There	53

Recovery	54
Begging	55
To Break Fast	56
The Moving Ons	57
Landmarks Made of Stone	58
Wash Rooms	59
Saving Room	60
Walking Home	61
Grooming	62
Space	63
The Things I Do for You	64
Lure	65
Acknowledgments	67
Author Biography	69

Do You See the Stars?

This is waking up. Remember
when you pressed your thumbs,
thick and unforgiving,
into my eye sockets? Slow as death
until I caved
to the dizzy and you whispered,
accent sticky, dripping in rose syrup,

Do you see the stars?

And I did. They burst in the darkness like kisses.
This city has a heart, fluttering
crazed and drunken as a beast, hands
itchy and always wanting, wanting
and a mouth with hunger so palpable
I gave myself in an instant. I was new,
damp when I came here, ridiculous
as one of those puppy mill survivors
too petrified to take a single step from the cage
into green grass and sunshine. I stumbled,
blinded,
but for the stars.

I risked it all for you
because it was home, because it was you,
the cage I left behind, dank and cloying
and so sadly, pathetically familiar. It was a husk,
forgotten like nightmares and used to be's,

but it was all I'd ever known.

Bad Indian

Bad Indian, not a speaker—who gives
a damn if they beat it out of my father
in residential boarding school? They say
"Pretendian" & an old man with creamed
blue eyes cackled after demanding my ancestry,

"Everyone's a Cherokee." I apologize

for green eyes, pale skin. It's not enough
to soften cries of "Wana'be clan!
Elizabeth Warren all over
again." Once an elder
vet spit on my wanting
cheekbones, my braids, that I didn't know
Lakota. I did not choose my skin

or the trauma curdling rancid
through my blood. We are born into creation
disasters, settled war zones, armed
with chanced defenses so forgive me

that ivory is my weapon. Poachers try
& they show teeth, dressed
in polyester & crafted altruism
but I am fast & I remember. I'm *kamama*, you really
think you got us all? We still roam
our land, thirteen thousand years is a single heart
beat in the whole story. I am telling you, listen:

I am hungry, matriarch
made too young. My grief's too big
to contain & like Damini I will starve
24 days to die from broken
chambers—and by god, how you will keen,
spill cracked-bone to your knees, pay
homage to my skeleton, to this bad Indian.

Spring Frenzy

Soon, it will be three, the deadest
of night. You, in trusting sleep, believe
I'm balled onto my side of the bed. Likely
dreaming of India and grinding
my teeth. You don't know
I'm here, beneath the alien light
listening to the drunks below
and devastated
we can never go back. When did it happen?
When did you start falling
asleep first, boiling water for rubber
bottles and shooting Rolaids
like cheap candy? What was the date
when we became happy
with grueling Uno games and dinners
without wine? Where did it go—
all that uncertainty and grabbing ons
of *just once mores*? We left it behind,
even the burned edges,
like shoes we outgrew or graphic tees
cracked with sweat. So many,
they don't come out together. They lose
grips in the haunted house, sight
of one another in the mirror mazes. But we,
we held tight. I followed your scent, you
listened for my breath and in the headache
sprouting bright of it all we've burst
like spring in frenzy smack into blossom.

Pulitzer Prize Pig

Pulitzer Prize Pig spoke of what it means
to be ***** as a ***** man with a look
the look   *that* look
women were born knowing
how to read. I knew
that look   *the* look
at fifteen when the AP teacher crouched
beside my desk in the dark
while flashes of syphilis
and gonorrhea shuddered
across the projector screen. (Still, even now,
I hear the tired clicking of the tapes.)
I knew the look,   saw *a* look,
at eleven when grown men whistled
at my unfolding hips and high
school boys rolled Corollas
along middle school parking lots
with eyes that spider-scurried
pressed breasts. And I knew, I saw
that look,   *his* look
at four. In the bathtub, I learned shame—
I shot my father
in the eye with a plastic alligator squirt
gun and never bathed with open doors again.
Pulitzer Prize Pig sidled up close, nosed for nipple
drinkers and sniffed out my slop. Trough walls
are low, but sticky, slick beside stys,
and boars are happy with scraps.

An Anorexia Thing

It's an anorexia thing, we watch
our hair fall like drunks, tangled between bony
fingers in the shower while the down
on our arms, face, chest flourish
in a sad attempt to keep us warm. We shake
like old women in apartments others call *roasting*
as they slip off their jackets so we can judge
the fat of their arms, slabs of flesh jiggling
fresh as meat on hooks. How thin
can I get before bones break
through skin? How little
must I weigh before I float down the streets,
a ghost to the masses, but an angel
to few? We don't talk
about it, but I recognize my own

and it's staggering in the war zone.

The Wrong Kind of Indian

I keep the smudged Pendleton blanket
nestled like a Christening gown in the hope
chest. It's green, smoked
with sage and cedar, blessed
by a medicine man beneath towering
tipi poles staked unnaturally permanent
into the earth. At the time

I didn't know washing the smoke over my body,
soaking it into my thirsty flesh, it wouldn't work
until years later. For a lifetime I kept myself locked
into my own hope, buried
in my own safe place, safe choices, safe
dullness. You opened it up greedily, treasures
tumbling like dismissed toys to the floor.

An elder brought you to me, all siren's smoke
and nature's magic—neither of us
are the wrong kind of Indian.
When Columbus found me, he thought he'd found you.
He was lost, reckless and foolish like us.
Then again,
what miracles, what marvels, wrong turns
and losing yourself can bring forth.

The Catamaran

May's long weekend was spent
on a catamaran in Manuel Antonio,
the crew's thick Jamaican tongues
twisting around Tico Spanish.
On the upper deck
I said I was leaving you
and couldn't look you in the face.
A dolphin laughed
and an Indian couple on their honeymoon
asked you to take their picture.
For three hours you tried
to untangle my reasons
until we both got sea sick
and spent the sunset hanging
our heads over the rails.

Resurrection

I never wanted to come back,
not here, where the mess sloshed over
like cocktails staining pretty satined feet.
I came back for you, happy
to leave the palm trees behind,
the howler monkeys on tin roofs.
Oregon is where it began, and the Great
Northwest demanded the act end here, too.
(That's always where the hook kicks in)
Moving on,
we'll leave the rain behind, the gummy
bars tired from our twenties, the restaurants plundered
and the rain-pregnant streets already forgetting
our stampeding feet. I returned
to check for a pulse, see if We
could be pulled back sharp
from the edge of extinction.
How glorious that our vitality
is alive and kicking wildly, strong
like something shot at close range
yet demanding stubbornly to live.

The L Words

I got up, still a little drunk, and ran
for miles after loving you. Sidewalks fell down,
verbs slammed against nouns, at four
in the morning when I'm leaving you.
My legs stretched 'til they broke, snapped
and tore with each stroke
and the sun—the sun
grooves into soberness
as I'm losing you.

Love You More

I sent you a keychain stamped *love
you more* from my crumbling
Costa Rican hacienda. You
were turning thirty and we
had years of regrets stitched
and scarred up and down
our arms like teenagers
in the grip of delusion, tired dogs
after the fights.
I waited

until you caught up with me
to say I was coming back,
my muscles tensed,
fat scars ropy thick, ready
for a blossoming explosion
black as your eyes swimming
beneath heavy brow
and deafening as your lips wrapped
like a vise around my name.

Totem of You

I've built a totem of you, hand carved
devotion—it filled my fingers with splinters,
my palms with gummy sap in the working wood

of loving you. That weekend at the Redwoods,
I slipped a piece of the Immortal Tree deep
into my denim. It's carried on a thousand years,
through the fires, the floods, bolts
of lightning and hungry loggers. It was like us,
solid through the storms, indifferent
to the whispers, stoic through the hard times.
Afterward, the guilt soaked in, heavy, fatty
and heady as rum cake. I buried the sacrifice
in the garden, gave it back to the Earth,
begged forgiveness of the Universe. But for you—

your totem is made of the branches of my mind,
the trunk of my body, the leaves of my heart.
Natives say the real beauty of the totem
is in the decay, the slow deterioration, the quiet
death we accept in comfortable silence. Not us,

for us the carvings will stay sharp, the etchings
forever unmoved. I built this monument with my everything,
a colloquy to where we've been
and the unshakeable of millenniums to come.

Childhood

Two memories from when I was three
define my mother and father. A bath in the chipped
tub bubbling from generous squirts of dish
soap that dried my skin. We could never
afford the real things.
The plastic horse squirt gun, half
full. My father came in
to shave his neck, swiping the blade neatly
around his moustache. When he finished,
he turned and scanned my naked body.
I shot him in the face,
scrubbed away his searching eyes and that
is how I learned what a gun is for.

I suckled my mother's breast until I could speak
because she wanted me to. The warm milk
filled my mouth, spreading to my limbs
like a drug. I lay on her chest in their bed,
a cartoon boxing match between a chicken
and a lamb on the TV. They squealed in one ear,
her heart beat in the other. As a bell rang and the animals
began circling, the nipple engorged
against my tongue, grotesque and huge, and that
is when I learned what teeth are for.
Years later, I watched my best friend's
five-year-old daughter
try to cover her mother's
chest with a blanket while her infant brother
was breast fed. A child discovers shame
as quickly as a farm animal
gets the metal bolt to the brain.

I Thought You Were Praying

Driving madly through the deserts outside Al Ain,
the baby sucking like a beast at your breast,
mosques gave way to dunes
and the Paki street workers to palms.
Beyond the camels,
past the tribesmen,
we didn't stop until we were away from it all—
the malls with their ungodly air conditioning,
the fat children making loud love to their sweets,
the fat wives engorged in their abayas, rolling
like sun-swollen beetles through the shops.
In ballet flats and the jeans that hugged my ass
like a fetish, I climbed the dunes as if I belonged,
while beautiful golden men in glorious keffiyehs
honked safely from the highway. And I,
staggering like a drunk
as the sand clung begging and desperate,
my cuckolded lover to my perfect white feet,
mounted the crest, dropped to my knees,
ready and eager as a whore,
to fil a mason jar with contraband. And you,
nipples burnished as the sand, laughed,
I thought you were praying.

Inside the Rosemary Bush

Early in the morning, while the tea is steeping,
I put out the ashtray full of seeds and bread
crusts for the quetzels and yigüirros.
The rosemary bush shakes underneath
the clothes I forgot to bring in from the line,
little fat brown balls roll out..
They have no shortage
of food, no predators, a backyard in Moravia
all for them. Their water pump to bathe
in, the *cas* tree dropping sweets
at their feet. This is what I left you for.
Watching overstuffed birds,
beggars tapping at the gates calling *upe!*,
the *huevos* man barking prices from a rusted van,
while I sit and write
page after page about you.

How I Like My Women

I like my women slight and frail, bones
hollowly light, ribcages pressed
like prison bars against the skin.
I love the women with stomachs caved in,
divots carved like ice cream scoops
below breasts begging to melt. It's the women
with the lips like readied blisters, skin sautéed
in good genes and creams
that remind me how exquisite we are
and of all I'll never be.

Men

There was the boy who asked *How
do I know it's mine?* before I had the carelessness
carved out. The one I left on impulse
after seven nothing years—who,
when I asked years later why
he didn't fight for me, said *I realized
you weren't worth fighting for*. Remember

the one who looked so damned good
at the bar in that across the room second—
the alcoholic I traded cries with, crumpled
in his medical scrubs? Then there was the man

whose dreadlocks whipped my arms raw, lucked
in with a visa lottery who fed me sips of rum
on our first date. His accent was lovely, heady
and congealed but still,

he wasn't you. You usurped them all,
needled deep into my meat, the organs,
into the weight of my bones,
the everything of all I had to give.

Christmas Chai

That Christmas I gave you an aphotic
steel teapot and you taught me
how to make chai.
I filled the gaping vessel's mouth with tap water
while you peeled slices of unwashed
ginger root. Two spoons
of Taj Mahal ground tea, a mouthful
for each.
Cardamom pods, cracked with your crooked teeth
and pried open with buffed nails, tossed
helpless in the boil. Milk
comes last,
an opaque white stream
soothing dark spiced water.

The sweetness we could never agree on.

My slow honey, your raw
sugar. That Christmas you gave me words wrapped
in a lilting accent and I taught you
how to say I love you.
I opened my mouth to take you in
while you peeled away clothes from the night
before to spoon,
together, on the mattress.
You bit my shoulder, red fissures from teeth
while I pulled your frenzied hair. Lost together
in the cheap red sheets,
I never came last.
And the sweetness
we could never agree on.

Relief

Us and every mammal on earth takes
twenty seconds to piss. Imagine that,
the great equalizer is between our legs
(of course). It doesn't matter
how many warm beers we forced down
during bumbling pauses at house parties
we never wanted to attend. If we just
got the trots training for a pointless race,
or held our bladders tight as a newborn
because the bathroom was too many
steps away (and we so lazy). We're the same
as baboons, house cats and cattle
being pointed to the slaughter house.
And that toilet paper? Those Turkish toilets?
The bidets, baby wipes and hoses
we swear never touched our asses? Those
don't make us better than the wild things
hunkered down, embarrassed,
eyes averted in the fields.

Bouquet of the Body

What they don't tell you about starvation
is that you hunger for nothing.
The pounds drop, an exhausted mother
lets go of a wailing newborn. Inches
slough away, calluses and tired skin
pumiced off with a burning stone.
I never once felt empty.
Instead, my stomach grew tauter,
crescent arrangements wilting beneath eyes
bruised and battered as wedding day gardenias
buried in creams and powders –
and my hip bones blossomed,
a quiet display of Asiatic lilies,
sickeningly sweet and nearly weeping
before the decay sets in.

Eating

A man makes love the way he eats, you
always devoured the *daal*
like a starving animal, thick fingers
yellowed with turmeric pinching
the steaming naan, over-ripened
lips slick with the juices of burst
lentils. Afterward, you did the same
to me, tearing at my flesh, hungry
and never sated. For years
I watched you suck and lap
up everything laid before you
until I realized I would never be
enough to satisfy the craving
that purrs within.

Hush-Hush

All my innards spill out in my writing, my words
pitifully ugly in the mess. But you, you have no leaks,
no *Oops what have I done*, no thrown
back laughs at the disasters. I can't find any cracks
in your frame, any chips in the armor or slits
amongst the shell. You say *I'm* the quiet one,
brimming with secrets and stuffed fat
as duck livers cum foie gras, luxurious
in the suffering and worth every gram. It's you
with the hushes, the shushing, furtive
side glances in the dark. You speak
when it suits you, an accoutrement
to indulgent stoicism, the dangling carrot
that brought me close. You want to see my insides?
The fallout from my storms? Here—
read this. Make yourself the main character,
the protagonist, my hero, my muse. These words
are for you, a sacrifice of my body and mind,
outlined in a crime scene's thick chalk
like a macabre display for the neighbors, fodder
for gossip and jokes as the world crawls on by.

Relativity

Cages are relative, the animals
showed me that. Gallops and scurries
from unclaimed Oregon wild
out back. Nightly, they came
for discount cereal, day-old
pastries, the scraps and crumbs
of our sorry offering. The skunks
groomed us to serve their favorites
earlier in winter, the raccoons
showed us they didn't like plates
or trays, thought they were traps,
proved they'd never miss a crumble.
The littlest ones, the babies,
the kits and fawns and joeys,
jolted with increasing confidence
towards the glass doors. Watched us
with curiosity as they feasted.
When we'd open the doors,
foots would stomp and tails went up,
rushings fast into the darkness
because we,
we were escaping. And we bolted
from our cage with a feral ferocity.

The Two Percent

Green eyes are the least desirable, that's
what studies in every country show. Makes sense
to me. My alligator eyes are hard to hold—people
look away. Ask if they're contacts. Say,
There's the Cherokee in you. They're too much
like a reptile, something cold to the touch
and lacking loyalty. Blue, that's where
the magic is. If your genes say *Nope, not for you*
and put cornflower on the high shelf,
brown will do. It's warm, like melted chocolate
and burns deep from the darkness. We like
what's normal. Common. To see ourselves
reflected back in our lovers' eyes.
Looking at me is like staring through twin
windows to a field of rich grass. Overwatered
even in the drought because I—
I don't give a damn if you're thirsty,
if your whiskey is too strong. I'll slurp it all
up to water my iris, let you press
your nose to the panes and gawk
at the selfish foreignness of my insides.

How Dying Is Done

They always tell you it's like a cancer, horse piss
spearing thick as butter into perfect alabaster,
but it's not like that at all.
When the black sickness began to crawl
up my arm, claws
dug in deep, inching up forearms
wrapped tight in veins.
The nurses and doctors were right,
It did look like cancer—but cancer,
it has more modesty
or shame than that. I watched it spread,
arching and keening like a crazed lover
while the doctors filed in, pudgy, tired penguins
telling me time and again
We don't know what this is, but this,
this is how dying is done.

We'll cut off the arm
to save the head and heart.
I'd heard that before,
year after knife twisting year,
but an amputation doesn't stop It.
Cuts aren't clean,
no matter who's wielding the scalpel.
God, I waited for the clichés, for the lights
or the montage or the regrets
to pour in as the monsoon,
but that's not how dying is done.

You keep on wanting
what your heart's been suffocating,
bearing down underneath blood and muscle, but still
It refuses to drown, what your head
turns away from, holding up ridiculous
mobiles and distractions that even a child
wouldn't fall for. You.

You were what I wanted
when the darkness set in, so furious and real
that It refused to stay buried like a guilt-soaked
secret. We'd grown into something so much heavier,
something of such Botero grandiosity,
that not even a vehicle as strong as my body
could keep it quiet or stop it from bursting into blossom.

Rezervations

I didn't grow up on the reservation, my Indian
summers were literal. The hot months gasped me in,
all pudgy pale legs and feet like my mom. My reservations
were in hushed English while the elders slipped through Cherokee,
sounding cool as hose water on worn yellow plastic. My name
was over-seasoned between warm brown lips, their eyes
crinkling with flavors of *doesn't belongs* and a dusting
of cruelty. Some relative I've forgotten
would translate at times, between snaps at the charred cob
and rheumy butter down the chin. They told me

I was reserved, too quiet, too white, and I left
my shoes on indoors. My first cycle rushed like a plague
the summer I turned twelve, a slaughtering, a whole
new Trail. I didn't tell anyone, shoved napkins
down my shorts, held my breath
through the rocky waves. My redness

is on the inside, something too precious
or filthy to let shine in the fiery Oklahoma sun. Now,

I make reservations in restaurants bursting
with pretenses, where deer
heart tartare is presented with boredom, a quivering
quail egg riding naked on horseback. Bison burgers are stacked high
with foraged berry glace and we call the fry bread
doughnuts, smother them with bacon or bright cereal
to go with the side of irony. I was never

one of them. But I pretend,
and I plait my hair, and I know my tribal
enrollment by heart. It's reserved permanent
into my hippocampus, real as Mom's high
arches, lingering as rusty stains on
underwear that chewed into slabs of thighs
struggling doggedly at the tired seams.

The Sweet Below the Bitter

I still want you to make me orange juice, to squeeze,
press and twist the rinds in your pillowy palms,
to make room
in the freezer because you know that's how I like it,
enceinte with pulp and buried in a layer of ice
I can crack as easily as your heart. I still listen
to the rhythm every night, the cycle of blood
and all the little things inside you
I'll never know completely—even if I wanted to, even
if I wasn't terrified of the fallout. Let me taste
the carpel, the sweet after the albedo bitter
and I'll drink it down not caring
of the trails like slugs left behind.

Kitchen Volcanoes

On the slabs we pull apart turkey carcasses,
you feed me diced paneer, wet and chilled, in nipped fingers.
It's where you make your evening mess, where I wipe
up your powders and crumbs, and where the lassi erupts
from our broken blender and bleeds
into the cracks and pores. Granite is an untamed thing—
volcanic, unpredictable, a force of a siren.
Deep in the magma chambers, melted rock oozes
and swirls. Sometimes the vile is spewed out in a bulimic fashion
but sometimes,
Sometimes,
it sits in wait for hundreds of thousands of years.
Rocks cool slowly like forgotten indiscretions.
Patience makes the heat forget, the boiling subside. In the end,
stoicism can erode a mountain, a volcano,

even you.

Lifetimes later,
granite rises to the earth's surface, scrubbed clean
and stone cold to strangers, children, everyone but us.
We make countertops from it, slice our dinners,

spill our drinks and break the glasses.

Great Grace and Sharp Wings

37 years old and still starving myself—how much
longer until I don't care anymore? You say,
Stop caring now, but I don't know
if I can be one of those old ladies
with limp hair and no lipstick.
(Not that this is old, it's just ...
when does old happen? How do we
simply slip into it like it fits? I'm not sure
I have the capacity to grow old
with grace or by any other means.)
Do we call fat 60-year-old women
fat-fat, or is that when plump begins?
How about 70? Or 80? When
does it all end and how do I stop
running hands over stomach
to see if today's a skinny day? My plan
is to die at 66, right before the life
insurance expires and maybe
(if I do it right) they'll say it was a slender
old woman who fell
with great grace and sharp wings
in front of that rumbling train.
There'll be no open casket, and guilt-
laden memories are kind to the dead.
(Please, if you remember, call me beautiful
in the obits and choose a photo
where my collarbones protrude like plumage).

The History in My Blood

Indian blood is precious, every
drop counts. Me, I'm whitewashed
so I lean hard
on that tribal card and papers
from the BIA. Look, here's proof!
Evidence of my Native-ness, and suddenly
I'm something special. I can go
to the free Indian clinic, get my teeth
polished with my blood. I picked up
a smattering of scholarships,
all little, but still
it was my descent that splattered
the applications. I check "other"
on all those forms that list White
Black Hispanic Asian and forget
about the Indians. Like
we were never here.
like we've forgotten. Ridiculous,
we remember everything.
It's here, in our veins, our arteries, rushing
to and from our hearts because we,
we're marked as Other. Different.
And they're thirsty for the red stuff.

Something Sweet

Do you want something sweet?
Your toddler came at me like a bacchanal,
mouth open with desire. Imagine
being that trusting, certain
that what was placed on your tongue would please,
the sugar grains scrubbing down your palate,
the ghee melting like perfection down your throat.

Kadri didn't know I called the *besan ladoo* sandballs,
that they required the perfect mix of chickpea
and *kadalai maavu*, that the *elachi* was the secret
or that you had to sieve the flour just right. All he knew

was that *sweet* was something good, that hands
were made for his pleasures. Imagine
being that naïve, the beauty in opening your mouth.

The Banana Plantation

Roberto passed a joint to me with sand-ploughed fingers
in the jungles miles above Limon while the others
did headstands inside between sips of wine
and rum from the bottles. Nobody talked
to Roberto—he was so beautiful
he stole your voice.
I didn't want to kiss him, I wanted
to memorize how he shook shells
as small as pinky nails from his dreads
and how his hip bones protruded like fins. *My father
says that the ocean will swallow
me one day, he said.* The woven hammock
chewed into my bare thighs while he perched
like a kingfisher on the porch rail
and told me how he worked
his father's banana plantation every morning.
The smoke filled my head as he rocked
me gently, burnished fist around hammock knots,
thick accent stumbling around foreign words
and all I could picture between his rolling r's
was the sunrise
surfing ritual, pink slipping from sky.
How his chest was chiseled
stone from the breakers. How the saltwater rutted
into him, shining off his shoulders,
even when the waters let him go, even
when his feet thrust into old Nikes,
even when it was time to weave
between the bushes, slipping
plastic *soda* sacks over one
bunch after another.

~~m~~URDERED & ~~m~~ISSING ~~i~~NDIGENOUS ~~w~~OMEN[*]

A girl gotta grow up, leave the rez, & do we talk about it? Igido called twice for bail but both were after a Tahlequah fall, & high with opioid they drove right through a gate. Bolted up the highway—bare feet & all—hitched a ride via lifted truck to take her far away before 911 with, *The devil up & took the car*. Dad left right outta jail, headed to the Pacific, & gave away that plot of Cherokee a year later. *You'da hated it* & I probably would have.

No folks gonna talk of them gone ones anymore. They look at me all, *Got some bless'n on y'all*—after all, no cop has got me (yet). No reason, really. Everyone else, the hole fam'ly, gone & sear to memory the creak of a cell's cot frame long ago. None of y'all can fathom at the places gonna call for me. They gone & settle prefrontal cortex, & that seems an okay place to some.

At 15, we 3 bunked all day 4 an aged wee-jee game: We'd all be dead by 23, and we laughed and made a bet 4 the chance. An ATV ate Ann at 18 and then a fancy cable hung by Althea came next. Hadn't even nudged me 4 that plan. And when death happen that way, we can't talk any decent way.

No one talk anythin' of funeral 1 or 2 & I kept lookout for a face I knew while the Catholic father went on & on about killin' another or you & prayin' for both. Father, what type of Native turn Catholic, anyway? Who tuck that in their brain? All thru junior year, neither talk of church or nothin'. Creator not have way to fix it, then?

Who up and say so long to that god? Why do NDNs stand for that nat'l song? So many of us wash away, walk away, drag and drug away, and nobody's com'n back from that havoc of war.

---

[*] This poem is written in a lipogram style, part of the oulipo family. The first stanza is missing the *m* in the phrase "murdered & missing indigenous women." The second stanza is missing the *u*. This pattern repeats as the stanzas spell out "murdered & missing indigenous women." (Once the poem has been read once, the missing letters continue to repeat by returning to the first stanza).

Some of us hate a couple, "wo," tacked to the 1st of what we call big boys. But with Tsaligi it's fixed—Asgaya, male. Agehya, female. Why make that "M" all a mess, wave wide those legs & smile? It's the 1st of the alphabet, debut of music, the call all of us made as we slipped to this place. & maybe that's the space us Agehya go to. The alpha, the basis, the middle of this wasted home.

I ran away, still a kid, and my mama said *why why why* until pills kick'd in. With my dad and sis, *Luv y'all* was last. With my mama, I try and say I try. I try. I try.

When they ask where we went, where we go, why gone permanent cloys & flanks so close, why holes & channels swallow w/ ease & no one asks or even seems to say that's strange, remember. Remember: those who are gone never go that far. We are here. We stay. To be forgotten means an agreement's complete—that's not ever gonna happen

&

Place Settings

I've never belonged at any table,
but I pass
the salt and looked up

which fork to use
in an etiquette book.

All my family's dead so nobody's
left that knows there's an Indian
girl with a sick head
who grew up poor and sometimes
likes to fuck women gone
and snuck into this little fête.
They don't look too close

because I got no color
and haven't been homeless
in years. Taught myself how to talk
right with sitcoms—these days,
I only slip up sometimes. Usually,
when the drinks kick in or in catching

the smell of a fellow interloper,
overlooked uninvited guest. And we smile,
tight lips coating teeth because a feast
is always better when it's free

and a gorging
always sweeter for the starved.

Constructing Carnage

A vine was choking the pine, throttling
its trunk and creeping up limbs.
Moss grew like pubic hair on the apple tree,
reaching past the heavy fruits to the earth.
The pear tree got it hard, plowed down
to make way for the extra wide driveway.
And the blackberry bushes? We paid
under the table to have them hacked to pieces,
annoyed at the berryblood splattering
the subfloors fresh from the mill.
For all the blessings, the *Pooja*, the cookies
given as bribes to new neighbors,
you can't cover up a massacre. There's no etiquette
that lets you pretend you didn't see.
Don't you hear the old growths screaming,
see the scared deer looking fruitlessly
for their loyal desire paths? In the forest,
where we built,
really we fit right in. What looked so lovely
in the morning mist—all Oregon green
and dewy grass—was an abattoir
the whole time. It's just,
now,
we're the ones cradling the pistols,
the guillotines, the saws
with teeth like sharks.

Racing Camels

Three women drove the Black Mambo
through the panting morning fog of Abu Dhabi,
dodging the Ferraris and Lamborghinis, the busses
tipped upside down and teeming with bloody workers
along the banks thick with red sand blown in like bullets
from the dunes.
We wanted to see the camels race.

On the outskirts of Al Wathba, young Arabs gathered at dawn,
urging their animals on, praying for the speed and heart
to catch the eye of the Sheikh, get a piece of themselves
tucked like another pretty bar of gold into the palace.
We were the only foreigners there,
the only women there
when the fog eased, an expert dom releasing his sub
seconds before the asphyxiation left a lasting mark
and the camels,
the camels,

they say they run for Allah, white spittle
soaping their mouths, but my god how they're ugly.
Legs too long and spindly to carry their refrigerator bodies,
all knobby knees and wavering humps
like they don't know their own carriage.
Like 14-year-old girls and in that,

suddenly they're beautiful.

The camels run with a deity's grace
and it doesn't matter that their bellies are thick
or their lips lift in the wind, baring crooked teeth
to the desert. We snaked along the tracks,
pacing the loping streaks until an old man wearing a hard face,
dishdash gritty with the sport, keffiyeh fighting the winds
pulled alongside us. We weren't supposed to be here,
but then again

the camels aren't supposed to know elegance,
to defy their bodies, to move like gods,
and so I waved to the Emirati, and in an instant
his hardness cracked, his hand lifted
and he burst into a smile bright enough to blow
the lingering gray to the universe. Three women
drove into the desert and found such glory
in a place so desolate even the beasts were exquisite.

Gestation

The sickest parts of me will always think
you wanted to adopt because of me. Imagine
a child with my alien eyes. Teeth too small
and jaw too wide. They'd be too quiet,
prone to fat, awkward
at birthday parties and chew
like a beast at their nails. Not once
would they smile for the camera,
and *Ungrateful!* would shoot
out my lips. They'd be too afraid
to think for themselves, turn
to you or me to answer the most obvious
of questions. *What do you want to be?*
Why are you so quiet? What in the hell
is wrong with you? They'd be just smart
enough to fake it for awhile, but slowly,
in time,
the averageness would struggle up
like a pimple. And I get it.
I wouldn't want me all over
again either. Is that what it is? Why you freeze
at the questions, were so unsure
of my birth control? Can you not fathom me
from the start, bear the terribleness
that dragged me, mute and shaking,
to where we are?

Down There

My eating has always been disordered,
distorted, disgusting. I willed the anorexia, you think
it really happens any other way? The researchers
point to all kinds of dumbness, call it
mental illness. Genetics. A side effect
of magazines. Does that explain being six
years old with a father who brings
Reese's every single day after work?
Buy my silence, fill my mouth so questions
don't leak out? What a deal
for just seventy-nine cents. How about
college, when I rounded up
like the blue-ribbon judges were coming,
got so fat all women and gay men could say
were, *Your tits look amazing!* And after?
When I got all normal? Don't think
that was an accident. Baby fat melting
like spilt Otter Pops on hot sidewalks? No—
it was a reflection of the latest disapproval,
my disappointment in myself switching
dressings again. What I put in my mouth,
what I keep out,
it's all the same. Stuffing, starving, stifling
it all down. My god, what's on the inside? What's
down there? What am I so scared
to let crawl up and out with curious
fingers and blinking wet newborn eyes?

Recovery

Recover is a funny word, like
what's buried that needs covering
again? What are we hiding in the dirt
and will the worms crawl through
my fingers, roots tear
at my cuticles or bugs catch
in my nails? We cover up a lot—
our thighs the size of calves,
the hip bone sawing into thin flesh
stretched taught as tanning
hides. Let's dig it up once more,
spread it out under fluorescent
lights and delight in the ugly of it all.

Begging

I've only begged twice, first
my father. Years later,
my husband. Both supplications
asked the same—to want me.
We're not dogs, women,
treats aren't balanced
on noses or scraps smuggled
under tables with our begs. Our tailbones,
they fused together years ago
during the blackouts of our twenties
when we stuffed our loneliness
with midnight pizza. No *good girls*
passed out or soft bellies rubbed
will answer our prayers
or satiate all the entreaties piled on
'til we pancake like busted
fighting dogs in the filth.

To Break Fast

Life crept back into me like a child
slipping into the Big Bed in the middle of the night. Slowly,
silently, so as not to disturb
the sleeping giants within. I was light
in a way starvation never allowed,
lucid,
the bony fingers of dangerous dreams slipping
off my shrunken arms. Just as nightmares
aren't welcome when a girl spoons close
to her mother's sleeping body, as they're scared
into submission by her father's monstrous snores,
my desire to vanish lifted like a morning stretch,
dissipating with a yawn at the pink, dawning light.

The Moving Ons

Today I was lonely
for you. For us, for what
it used to be. The Nehalem
days are over, the nights we'd careen
upon one another with other people,
then into each other after last calls.
Tonight I was lonely for the desperate
hopes of used to be's. We grieve sadness
just as much as happiness, as deeply
as love, as hard as the worst days.
Just now, I'm lonely
even with you right by my side, steady
through the comforts, wailing inside
as I curl up my feet and you stroke your moustache,
confident in the familiarity while I grasp,
drowning and desperate, oceans away.

Landmarks Made of Stone

I remember when forty was old, when
I was sure I'd escape the cancer,
when I thought my mother was beautiful. Remember

when the creak of your jacket sang like whales,
your skin soft as whipped butter
and my lips a feral ground
undiscovered? We were kids,
the lot of us, allelomimetic
but thinking we were the first. Nobody
from nowhere had found such fortunes—

quick, bury it again, hands clasped fast,
fingernails clawing through dirt
before the world sees what we've found.
Together, we'll bury our gems,

stash the gold and erect a cairn
only we'll remember the shapes of. Oval
and smooth, round with river-hewn
edges. And this one,
the jagged one, the one with obsidian
stretch marks in the igneous. This one

we'll know as ours through the blindness,
the aging, the total
fall-apart of our cocoons.

Wash Rooms

That night I laid across the washing
machine for an hour, to keep
the bad wiring from shutting it down, I thought—

most women would be enjoying
a raucous, machine-gifted orgasm.
And I remembered
the man I read about in Williamsburg,
the one

who rented a crawl space above a theater
for $450 a month. He had to stoop
to save his head and pitied
how he could never bring home a girl.
I thought

I could live here. You know? Here,
in this closet of a room
where my bed would quake
like a fault line and water gurgled
below my hips. My body was enough

to stop the mistakes, still the beast
and turn the makings of my draperies
clean, clean, clean.

Saving Room

A dessert too sweet? That's nonsense
even as a child I never believed.
Give me the corner piece, buttercream
piled high in shells and roses,
Corneli lace by the foot and sotas for days.

I'd scoop out the cake, an unnecessary social obligation
like dinner before your mouth on mine,
whiskey before shirts on floors,
and feast on sheer frosting, grains crashing against my teeth
rough as the tide—this

is still how I like it, creamed nipples
and syrup on collarbones, rivering down,
down,
into the devil's food of our bodies
moist and molten in a way
fondant artists and bakery slaves
never imagined pulling from the heat.

Walking Home

You told me your grandfather would pick you up from school,
homemade *naan* in hand or a melting ice cream cone. The walk
from the gated walls to the family home
took minutes, yet in those tired trudges—Mumbai heat
raining down, you ate somnambulism, his papery hand
engulfing yours. As a child,
you were the biggest, school uniforms
custom made, limbs swollen with sweets,
belly thick with *paratha* and *ghee*. You tell me
you don't remember the walks home, the pieces
torn with teeth, the sticky melting
trails along your chin. After hours of English
stuffed down your throat, cricket in the yards
and burrowing your role as eldest son deep
as *golgappi* centers, you didn't notice anymore
that the shoes pinched your feet, constraints
too tight to contain your otherness. And now
decades later,
the fat melted away, the hunger's spirit broken,
subdued, all I see of your childhood
are those pinky toes tiny, stunted,
adornments on your massive puppy feet.

Grooming

You clip your nails like one does a child's, I hear you
in the bathroom between the local news breaks
and trumpets from the stadium across the street. To the quick,
toeing across the free edge, your fingernails are all fresh
cuts and uneven trims. It's here,
in these moments,
when you emerge down the hallway,
every stray piece of you swept up neat in bins, I imagine
how you used to be. Before America, when your grandmother
would snip at your fingers carefully, dreaming up half moons
and stories dipped in magic. Afterward, each digit was battered
in *ghee* and sweet jams, plucking at *parathas* and wiping
up *dahl*. I've always adored your hands, the histories
they cup into the plunging, echoing crevices and the empty
crags begging to be filled with squeezes and pinches of me.

Space

As children, two oceans
separated us, the Pacific flirting up my legs
hungry as a frantic demon
on those frigid coastal trips. The Atlantic
cloyed like a diseased and desperate
lover close to your family
home in Mumbai. Twenty years ago
neither of us would have believed
it would all come down to Us—you,
a child playing cricket in the streets,
me plotting my escape from that smothering
small Oregon town, and We,
what we found was unsinkable, for good,
a buoy no ocean dare drown.

The Things I Do for You

The things I do for you
are without thinking,
no scores kept or favors stacked.
It's in the simplicity, the ease
that I know now—as I always have—
that loving you is natural, as much
a part of me as my crooked eyebrows.
That's why

I give you the good pieces
of bread, the thickest morsels
torn from cookies, the water
with the least ice (I know
how you hate the cold.)

My heart is threaded
into these gestures. Without thought
yet over-seasoned with adoration

are the things I do for you.

Lure

The grace and urgency in the chaos hooked me hard,
a hungry and stupid fish
flailing in the sudden lightness of it all,
amidst heavy boots and stomping accents.
I was terrified,
never good at taking tests, and this,
this is what it all came down to.
I smelled nothing of the open sewers,
my heart cracked no more at the grasping
of child beggars, unwilling to explode into confetti
even after all the beatings
you'd given it for five thirsty years.
The heat didn't suffocate or burn,
but wrapped my slight body like a blanket—
for once in my life I was warm.
But it was the secrecy, the touch prohibition
that sparked in me what we'd let go dormant
in the pressing Oregon gray,
the squeeze of a thigh
in the backs of rickshaws,
the kissing of fingertips
when sharing street *paan*,
the non-accidentals that made me love you
over and over and all over again. And that night,
dosas on banana leaves, daal in silver tins
while I commanded my left hand to stay,
pale and slippery as an exocoetidae
in my lap while I downed the spiciest dumplings,
the most searing soups, I swallowed the heat
of 1,826 days until my lower lip split open,
copper slicing fillets down my throat.
You took me to the falooda stand
where the heavy cream licked my wounds
and the mosquitoes tore my legs apart.

I didn't care
about the dengue or malaria or the ugliness
of the unknown, all I knew
is that my body's always betrayed what my insides hunger after,
and maybe the fish aren't such idiots after all, maybe
they just know what their desires are worth.

Acknowledgments

"Bad Indian." *Rising Phoenix Review,* July 2018.

"Spring Frenzy." *The Long Island Literary Journal*, October 2017.

"Pulitzer Prize Pig." *Pennsylvania English*, December 2018.

"The Wrong Kind of Indian." *Hawaii Review*, September 2017.

"The Catamaran." *Coldnoon Poetics*, Nov. 2012.

"Love You More." *Commonline Journal*, 2013.

"Childhood." *The Cossack Review*, June 2013.

"Inside the Rosemary Bush." *Speculative Edge*, Nov. 2012.

"How I Like My Women." *Projected Letters*, July 2018.

"Christmas Chai." *High Desert Journal*, Oct. 2012.

"Relief." *Clumsy Quips*, September 2017.

"Bouquet of the Body." *L'Allure des Mots*, Feb. 2013.

"Eating." *The Missing Slate*, Feb. 2013.

"Relativity." Ed. AEleen Frisch. *Microtext 3*. Wallingford: Medusa's Laugh Press, 2018.

"The Two Percent." *Yellow Medicine Review*, Mar. 2016.

"How Dying Is Done." *Red Savina Review*, 2014.

"Rezervations." *The Elephant Magazine*, Feb. 2017.

"Great Grace and Sharp Wings." *Sheila-Na-Gig*, June 2019.

"The Banana Plantation." *Speculative Edge*, Nov. 2012.

"~~mURDERED & mISSING iNDIGENOUS wOMEN~~." *HCE Review*, April 2019.

"Place Settings." *The Pangolin Review*, September 2018.

"Down There." *Urban Sasquatch*, Mar. 2016.

"The Moving Ons." *Leaping Clear*, March 2018.

"Landmarks Made of Stone." *Roar: Literature and Revolution by Feminist People*, September 2017.

Author Biography

J.C. MEHTA is a multi-award-winning poet and author of over one dozen books. She's currently a poetry editor at *Bending Genres Literary Review*, Airlie Press, and the peer-reviewed *Exclamat!on* journal. During 2018–19, she was a fellow at Halcyon Arts Lab in Washington, DC, where she curated an anthology of poetry by incarcerated indigenous women and created "Red/Act," a pop-up virtual reality poetry experience using proprietary software. As a citizen of the Cherokee Nation and native Oregonian, place and personal ancestry inform much of Mehta's creative work.

Mehta's novel *The Wrong Kind of Indian* won gold at the 2019 Independent Publisher Book Awards (IPPYs). Mehta has also received numerous visiting fellowships in recent years, including the Everett Helm Visiting Fellowship at the Lilly Library at Indiana University at Bloomington and the Eccles Centre Visiting Fellowship at The British Library. Visual representations of her work have been featured at galleries and exhibitions around the world including IA&A Hillyer in Washington DC and The Emergency Gallery in Sweden. Mehta is a popular speaker and panelist, featured recently at events like the US State Department's National Poetry Month event, "Poets as Cultural Emissaries: A Conversation with Women Writers," as well as the "Women's Transatlantic Prison Activism Since 1960" symposium at Oxford University.

Mehta is also the owner of a multi-award-winning writing company and founder of the Jessica Tyner Scholarship Fund, the only scholarship exclusively for Native Americans pursuing an advanced degree in writing. She has undertaken poetry residencies around the globe including at Hosking Houses Trust with an appointment at the Shakespeare Birthplace Trust in Stratford-Upon-Avon, England and the Acequia Madre House in Santa Fe, New Mexico. Her doctoral research focuses on the intersection of poetry and eating disorders.

Learn more about J.C. Mehta's work at www.jessicamehta.com.

www.ingramcontent.com/pod-product-compliance
Lightning Source LLC
Chambersburg PA
CBHW030132100526
44591CB00009B/620